Patchwork
Picture
Dictionary

Written by Felicia Law
Illustrated by Paula Knight

Published by Mercury Junior

butterfly

cat

snail

animals

tiger

elephant

parrot

dog

fish

zebra

rabbit

frogs

clothes

rubber boots

dress

shoes

sock

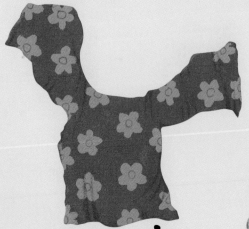

sweater

trousers

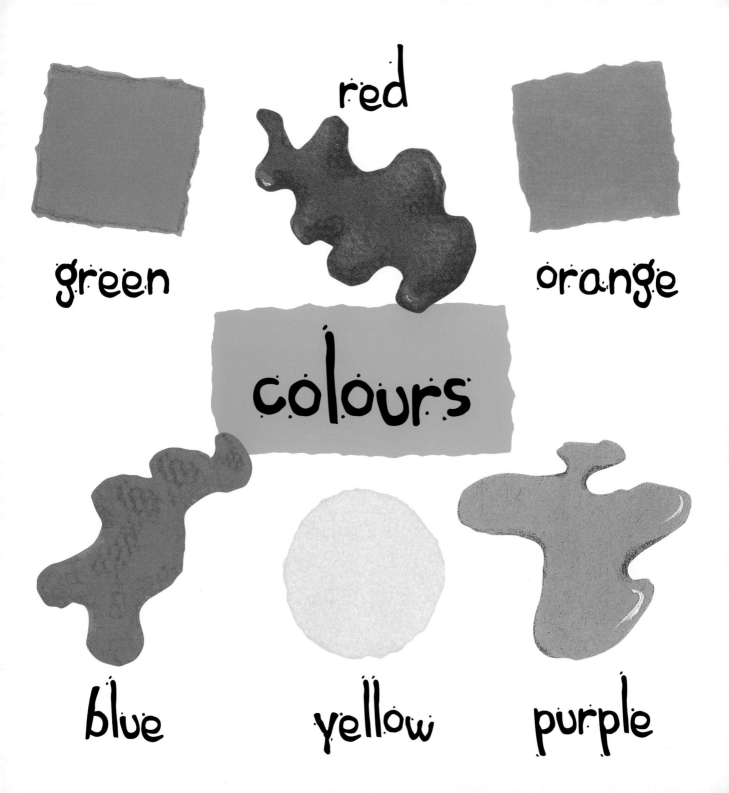

green

red

orange

colours

blue

yellow

purple

zero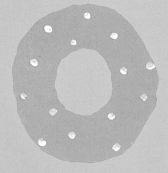

 one

two

numbers

three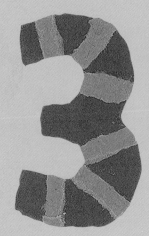

 four

five

six

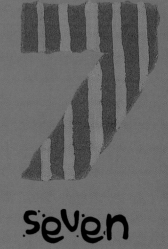
seven

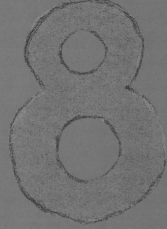
eight

nine

ten

tomato

ice cream

doughnut

food

cake

bread

gingerbread man

drink

cherry

candyfloss

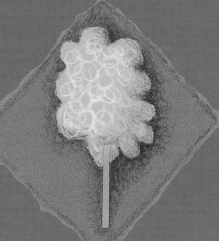

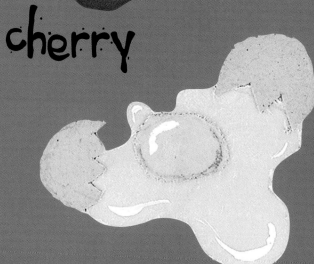

egg

shapes

square

triangle

circle

heart

rectangle

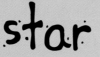

star

tree

flower pot

cactus

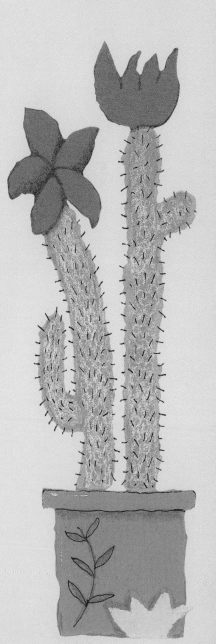

plants

lily

sunflower

home

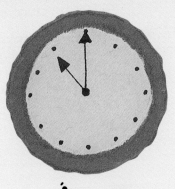

clock

house

chair

table

bin

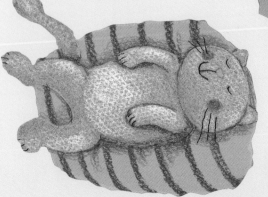

cushion

in the kitchen

mug

rolling pin

jug

plate

apron

pepper pot

grapes

apple

orange

grapefruit

fruit

melon

banana

fun and games

snowman

dancing

paddling pool

juggler

diving

moving about

aeroplane

tractor

pushchair

bicycle

scooter

van

tricycle

skateboard

sledge

music

trumpet

violin

tambourine

drum

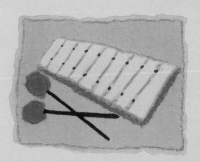

xylophone

my face

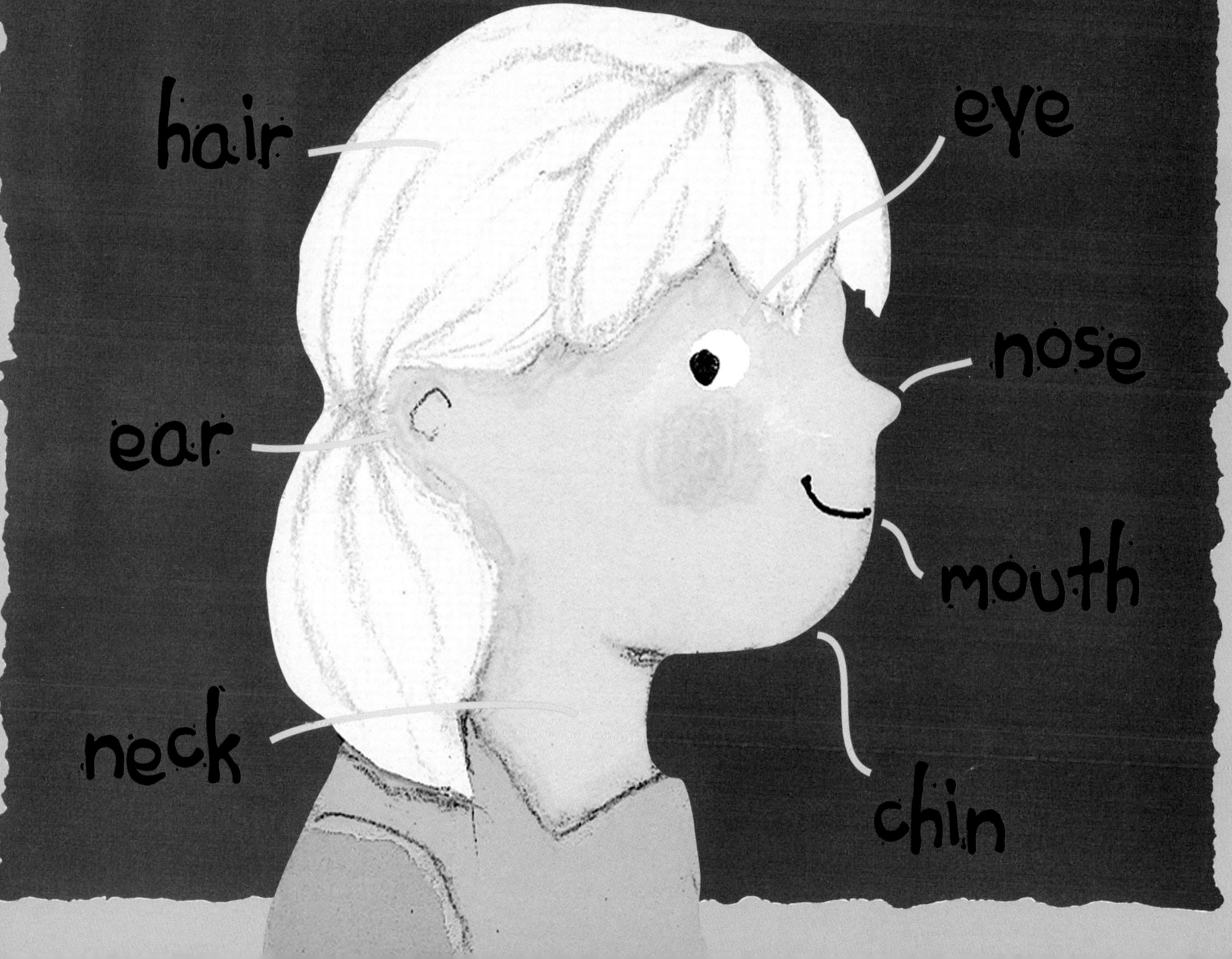

hair

eye

nose

ear

mouth

neck

chin

balloons

book

doll

toys

teddy bear

bricks

ball

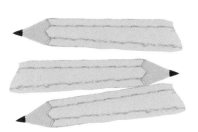

pencils

jigsaw

paints

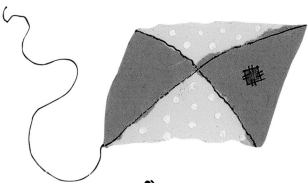

kite

family

mum

sisters

brother

dad

uncle

grandpa

aunty

granny

Mercury Junior

20 BLOOMSBURY STREET
LONDON WC1B 3JH

This edition published 2005 by
Mercury Books
20 Bloomsbury Street
London WC1B 3JH
ISBN 1-904668-86-0
Copyright © 2003 Allegra Publishing Ltd

Printed by D 2 Print Singapore